CREATING MEMORIES AT WOODLOCH

A Publication of Milk & Cookies Press
a J. Boylston & Company, Publishers imprint

MILK &
COOKIES
PRESS
TM

CREATING MEMORIES AT WOODLOCH
Text Copyright © 2023 by Therése Palmiotto
Illustrations Copyright © 2023 by Samuel Palmiotto

J. Boylston & Company, Publishers
Manhanset House, Dering Harbor, NY 11965-0342
www.ibooksinc.com
ISBN: 978-1-899694-xx-x
First edition, hardcover printing: 2022
Library of Congress Cataloging-in-Publication Data available

CREATING MEMORIES AT WOODLOCH

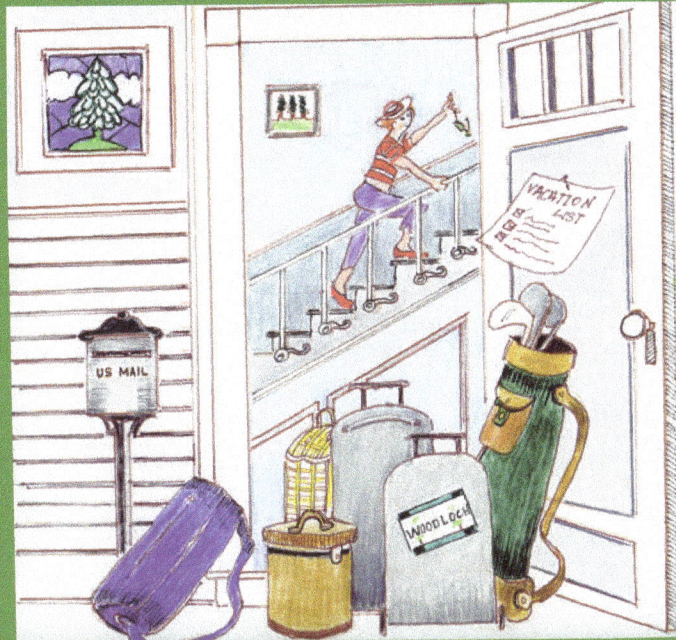

written by Therése Palmiotto
illustrated by Samuel Palmiotto

MILK &
COOKIES
PRESS
™

New York
Habent sua fata libelli

VACATION LIST

US MAIL

WOODLOCH

4

Our luggage is packed,
the car is ready to go,
We're in vacation mode!

We'll know we've really made it,
when we get to
Welcome Lake Road.

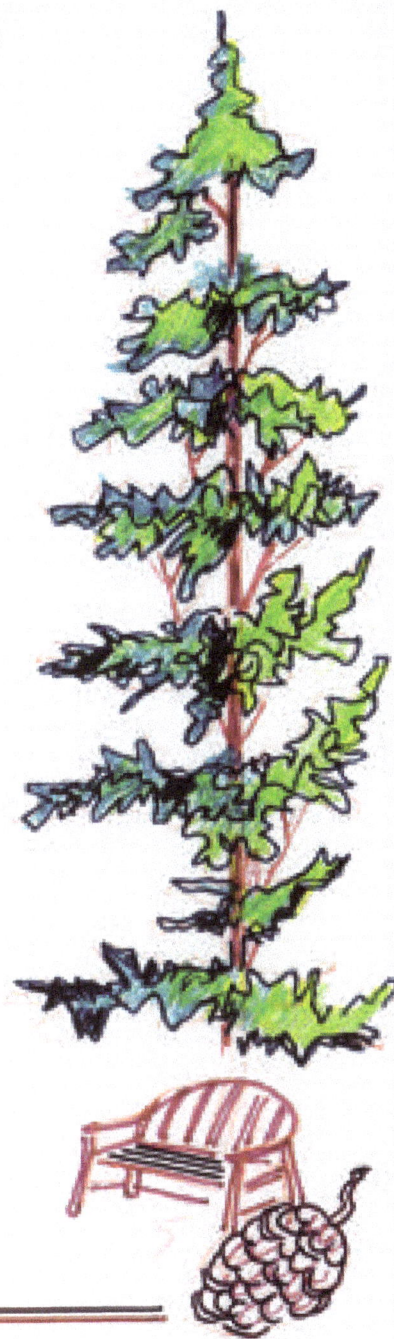

The first stop is at Reception.

Front desk staff
will welcome you there.

It's fun to pose for a
picture with...
but do not climb
on the bear!

WOODLOCH

PLEASE
DON'T
CLIMB
the
BEAR

Fun games & family
competition...
included in your stay.

Don't forget
to check the schedule.
The activities change
every day.

Bumper cars and go-carts.
Try the climbing wall
if that's your thing.

Swing the string towards
the hook.
See if you can catch it
on the ring!

Scandinavian pancakes...
or the famous crumb cake.

If you sleep too late
in the morning,
missing breakfast
would be a mistake.

1958

OPENING DAY WOODLOCH!!

Let's remember
Woodloch's founders,
Mary & Harry Kiesendahl.

They came in 1958...
and started it all.

WOODLOCH
PENNSYLVANIA
300 ACRES

SPRING

AUTUMN

SUMMER

WINTER

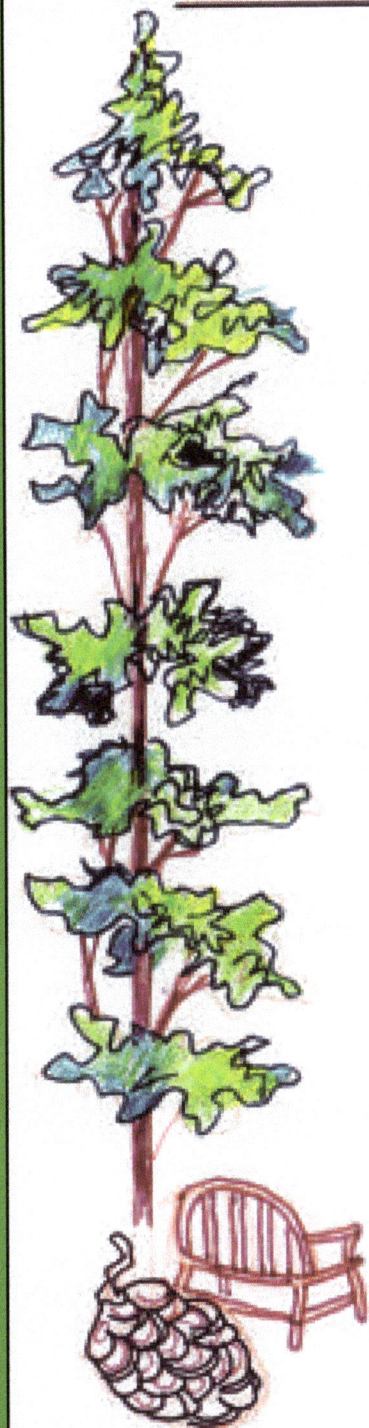

Since then
Woodloch has expanded...
a four-season family resort.

The Pines span over 300 acres
With accommodations
that never come up short.

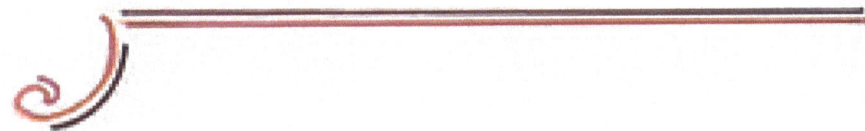

Greenbriar, Mountain Laurel...
or rooms in Spring Brook—

Rooms feature
stunning lake-views...
and balconies to overlook.

Try to win one of the medals...
in Family Feud or Double Dare.

Scavenger Hunt or Bakery Wars...
each one a fun family affair.

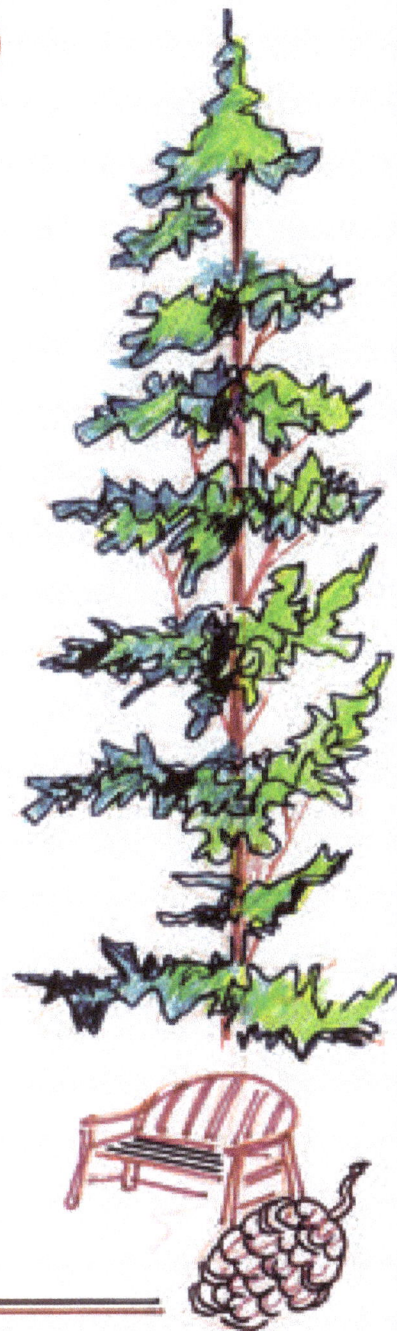

The Boomer Cub Club...
is for the younger crowd.

Arts and crafts,
story-time competitions—
but only kids allowed!

BOOMER
Cub
Club

PASTE

CRAYONS

I ♥ WOODLOCH
4 EVER

LAKE TEEDYUSKUNG SHOW

Enjoy Lake Teedyuskung.
Jump right in or
go down the water slide.

Sailboats, pedal boats, kayaks
or canoes...
waterskiing for your
adventurous side.

There's nightly entertainment....
You'll be impressed
if you choose to go.
Magicians and comedians,
Or the Broadway-style theme show!

WINNER
1

BINGO

7

3
3

FAMILY & FRIENDS

OLYMPICS !

Get your Bingo cards ready....
Pick your favorite
horse in the race.

Maybe in the
Family Olympics....

Your team will come
in first place!

At night when
it's time to turn in...
you've had the 'best day ever!'
but it's done...

Sleep sound and peacefully...
because tomorrow
will be another one!

Each visit is
special and unique...

whether you are there
to relax or celebrate.

Cherish all of the
Woodloch traditions...
and the memories
that you create.

Dedicated to

Margaret & Bill Fehringer,

the grandparents that built a

foundation of generosity,

focusing on the importance of

family and celebrating the value

of laughter.

Milk & Cookies Press
Manhanset House
Dering Harbor, New York 11965-0342
www.ibooksinc.com

www.IngramContent.com

For sales in the UK and Europe please contact our distributor,
Gazelle Book Services
Falcon House, Queens Square
Lancaster, LA1 IRN, UK
Tel: (01524) 68765 Fax: (01524) 63232
stef@gazellebooks.co.uk

www.ingramcontent.com/pod-product-compliance
Lightning Source LLC
Chambersburg PA
CBHW040852100426

42813CB00015B/2786